SURVIVING THE STORM

The Storm Is Passing Over

Psalm Okpe

SURVIVING THE STORM

Okpe Psalm Fresh Oil Ministry Int'l Church 133, Egbeda - Idimu Road, Egbeda, Lagos, Nigeria

Tel: 2348137015966

E-mail: godsubmarine@yahoo.com

Website: www.freshoilinternational.org

Copyright(c) 2009 by Okpe Psalm

Published by Parchment House Company Lagos, Nigeria

Designed & Printed by Brooks & Capital Lagos, Nigeria

All scripture quotations are taken from the King James Version of the Holy Bible, unless otherwise stated.

ALL RIGHTS RESERVED.

No part of this book may be reproduced without the express written permission of the author who is the copyright owner.

TABLE OF CONTENTS

Contents

TABLE OF CONTENTS 3

DEDICATION 4

ACKNOWLEGEMENT 5

INTRODUCTION 6

CHAPTER 1 8

I SAW THE FOURTH MAN LIKE THE SON OF GOD 8

    HELP, I'M DRYING UP! 8

CHAPTER 2 21

OH GOD WHY AM I HERE? 21

    Wait in His Presence 23

CHAPTER 3 31

DON'T COME IN, I'M NAKED! 31

CHAPTER 4 45

FIRMNESS UNDER FIRE!..45

CHAPTER 5..59

The God Who Married A Tramp..59

OTHER BOOKS BY THE AUTHOR 64

ABOUT THE AUTHOR..65

DEDICATION

I DEDICATE THIS book to my friend of the heart Rev Ernest Thunder Bolt in England. You were there for me during trying times and troubled waters. Also to J.T Frankly, when you didn't even have much you gave me all to prove how much you loved me. Mc Albert in Sweden you are my twin brother indeed. Bishop Morgan you are more than a brother; it was nice preaching in your church in Madrid, Spain. To my covenant friend pastor Clement Eriakha, thanks for having me on your platform while in Paris, France.

ACKNOWLEGEMENT

MY APPRECIATION GOES to the GOD of all creation who watches over me from a great distance and who brought this work to my heart. You are God over all and I love you Lord! To my pastors, staff and members of Fresh Oil Ministry International Church, It would not have been possible without you all. To my kids and my lovely wife Lydia, I'm proud of you more in these years of working with you; I have found you more than a help meet. Stay strong in the grip of God's love and always remember that He is the GOD WHO MARRIED A TRAMP!

INTRODUCTION

EVERYDAY WE ARE FACED with decisions and choices to make and depending on how informed, proud, arrogant, religious, weak or strong, greedy, emotionally stable etc we take steps that more often than not, get us into quagmires. As we consider what to do or try to get extricated, we find ourselves getting even more messed up. Some people would cry 'help I'm drying up" others would ask "Oh God why me, why am I in this situation" others still, in shame would try to cover up by keeping everyone at arms length "lest anyone come close and see my nakedness." This book aimed at both those suffering, and those God has placed in a position to help them, tries to let everyone know that God has no favorites, that no matter a man's social status, pedigree, or messed up situation, God still loves him and wants him as His bride. We are born of a sperm that can not be destroyed and it's the sperm of God which is His word and His spirit. This means that we are indestructible and is no situation, circumstance or storm of live that is strongenough to destroy a Christian. This is the truth because the bible says so ... Being born again not of corruptible seed but of incorruptible by the word of God that lives and abides forever. Stop the anxiety, stop the fear, the storm is passing over ... for the things which we see are temporary the persecution is temporary, the affliction is temporary the failure is temporary, the childless marriage is temporary, the marital trouble is temporary, it may last one week, one month, one year or more but you are of an indestructible sperm and the storm is passing over now.

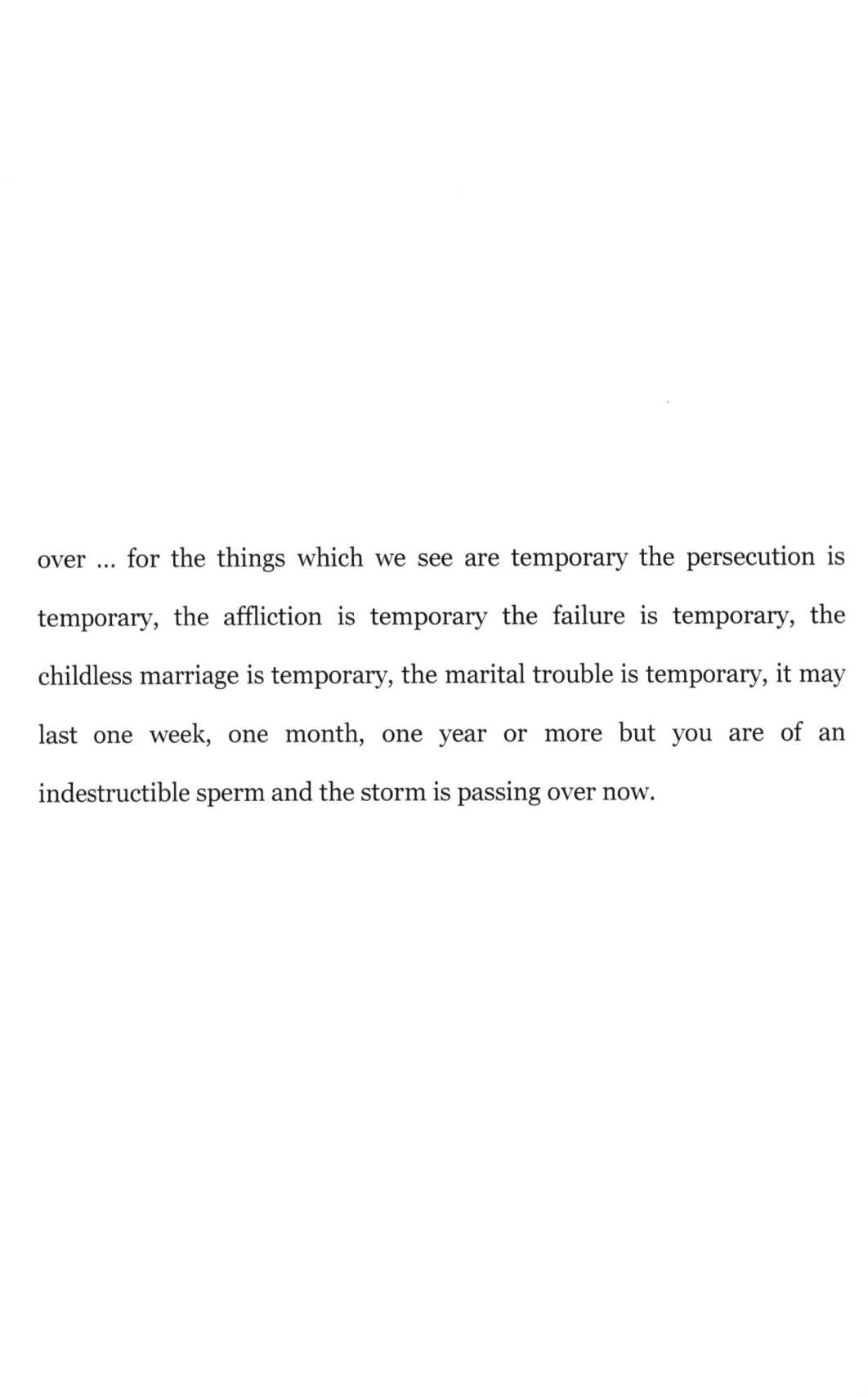

CHAPTER 1

I SAW THE FOURTH MAN LIKE THE SON OF GOD

HELP, I'M DRYING UP!

Talk about a bad day!

Helen woke up with a pounding headache. It felt like a thousand zealous carpenters were all hard at work in her head at the same time. A single mother, her daughter had been feverish, crying and tossing all through the night. She had to stay awake, watching over her and only dosed off when the baby calmed down at about a quarter to five. She was sure her eye lids had not touched each other when her alarm went off at five-thirty. She trashed around with her hands until she located the nuisance and shut it off, but sleep had fled. That's when she noticed the carpenters banging with the murderous intent of shattering her head. She stood up with a groan. As she tried to organize her thoughts in preparation for the business of the day, her phone rang; she picked it up and was told to hurry down because her shop was on fire. She rushed out, shouting as she went for her younger sister to watch over the baby. She got into her car but the car wouldn't start. She got out and started running, but that only increased the zealousness of the workmen in her head. She tried to ignore the ache, but the pain was already making her dizzy, so she closed her eyes and stopped. When she opened her eyes she was lying on her back, in a hospital bed, with bandages every where across her body except her eyes. Slowly she turned her head which felt heavy as lead, though without the blinding pain that assailed her earlier, and at the far end of the wall she could see a wall clock, and the hands if they were to be trusted indicated it was six o'clock. Just then a male nurse came walking by, and she beckoned on him 'Ah I see you have regained consciousness; let me get the doctor at once'

'Wait' she said 'before you go for the doctor, is that clock over there correct?

'Yes' answered the nurse.

'So I've been here for like how many minutes?'

'Minutes? You've been unconscious all day madam. Now just relax and let me go get the doctor' at which he hurried off. It was the doctor who explained that she had stopped in the middle of the road and was knocked down by an oncoming vehicle. A kind passerby brought her to the hospital and paid for her treatment. Her phone was smashed in the accident, so they could not try tracing her relations when she was unconscious. She borrowed the doctor's phone, called her sister and was told they had all been trying to reach her to no avail, the shop was razed to the ground, the landlord had brought them a quit notice, and baby's fever had become so high she had to take her to the hospital; she was on admission. The phone fell from her Helen's hand and clattered to the floor as she closed her eyes and settled back into unconsciousness.

How do you survive those days when bad news like those in need of miracles wait in line just to talk to you? How do you handle a day that from the word go, seems to have taken on a mind of its own, gone crazy, and is bent relentlessly on ruining all you have labored for so long to build? What do you do when the child of your very loins says "I hate you!" calls you a witch, tries to frustrate or kill you? How do you get back on your feet after your spouse announces, "I just can't live with you any longer"? How do you face your congregation when your old girl friend appears in church on Sunday morning with a baby in her hands claiming it's your child, the product of your covered sin? How do you resurrect hope when the doctor says "am sorry, but there is no hope"? Do you feel the need to just give up, lie down and die, when the disastrous floods of life's vicissitudes threaten to sweep away the very foundation of your life, leaving the stench of mold in the place of the fragrances of flowers?

If bad news has closed your in-box, you are obviously not alone. You may find it hard to imagine or believe it but I dare to say, you are about to discover a restoration! Everyman has his own mountain, tailored to his size. Job had to deal with his mount Everest-like problems, and even when he didn't know why so many terrible things where happening to him, he some how managed to trust God's love for him, and he came out tops.

Every hero and heroine in the bible had to persevere through tough times. We often encounter the same type of situations each of them faced. The question haunts our minds; will we survive, much less thrive?

I SAW THE FOURTH MAN LIKE

THE SON OF GOD (Daniel 3:25)

It's amazing to know that God is with us strong and mighty even when we feel deserted in the mist of adversities, afflictions, struggles, failures, sickness, trauma. For He has said I will be with you to the end of the world and in another place He said I will not leave you or forsake ... ***when you go through the waters, it will not drown you and when you go through the fire it will not consume you.*** But how many of God's children maintain this consciousness in the heat of live troubles and boldly declare that my God is strong and mighty with me and I can't be consumed for that which I go through today is passing away for many are the affliction of the righteous but the Lord delivers from them all. Hallelujah! This is the mentality and consciousness that will bring you out of whatever affliction you are going through in life.

From the scripture above, the three Hebrew boys dared the most dreadful King on earth at the time; they demonstrated their confidence in the God of their father Abraham, Isaac and Jacob the ancient of days and the Monarch of the Universe but it didn't seem like God was with them, they didn't feel any sensation to prove that He is present .God didn't do anything to stop or change the mind of King Nebuchadnezzar. A lot of times God is calling us for a higher walk of faith with Him beyond the conventional ways we have known Him and many get confused, discouraged and fainted when God isn't through yet. Many never want to be shifted from their comfort zones, they have become elastic to God; they will always withdraw to the old self. God wants to introduce new Signs and Wonders to the world through you. You have not known anyone who have gone through it or through that path and made it or return, but God wants to defy that philosophy by using you for Signs and Wonders, all He needs is your confidence in His Love, Power and Faithfulness to the end. God didn't stop the king or change his decision and God didn't stop or quench the fire as they maintain their confession of faith, O King, we will not bow! They thought they were making the furnace hot enough for their rudeness but the consuming fire Himself had appeared in that fire and had consumed the fire they had set-up and He was the fire in the furnace that received them and showed Himself to the King as the fourth man in the fire. **For He is the one that baptize with the Holy Ghost and with fire. Halleluyah.** God wants to be with you in the fire and even when you go through the flood.

Mere thinking that God would just stop you entry the fire is not good enough and that won't change anything or your situation. What you need is not just discussion or words of philosophy that would just make you feel calm or cool about the situation; **what you need is change!**

Many of God's children would murmur, complain, cry and look unto God to do something and when nothing seems to happen they get mad with God and everyone around them. First, you must know God and be consciousness of His strength with you.

Secondly, you must know what He has said concerning you and that situation. You must know and have His word for that circumstance because His words reveals His will and His judgment.

Thirdly, when you know and have His word for that circumstance then He has made you a god and judge over that trouble and you have got to proclaim the word and when you do, it is God judging that situation through you and like the wall of Jericho fell whatever that trouble is, will fall without resistance.

I DECLARE TO YOU A MYSTERY

Brothers and sisters, today I declare to you a mystery; that those walls of limitations, afflictions, sickness, failures, lack, poverty, whatever they are, that they are not real, God has remove their foundation in the realm of the spirit, they are walls without foundation, they appear real, those who recognized them never move on with God and in live but the few who believe God and His word, those who say if God said move on then I've got to move on; are those that become wonders to their world.

When you go close to them, they will fall down flat but as you go on there are other walls you are going to encounter in your walk in live there are some that when you come meet, they will not fall, what you do to these kind of walls is to push them down, there are some that you have to jump over and there are some that you have to close your eyes and refuse to recognize them and keep walking towards them and you will eventually walk through them, praise God!

This is the type that the Hebrew boys were faced with. When we study God's word, we would see how God has walked with men in the Bible days and this would give us an understanding of the person that is with us and the kind of God we are serving, sometimes God wants to mock and make jest of our adversaries in a very ridiculous manner and He wants us to see, think and act like Him because we are His offspring, that's what the Hebrew boys did.

MEET LAZARUS

I know of a man who probably felt like you do; in the gospel of John, the eleventh chapter, we meet a man called Lazarus, a man known as the friend of Jesus. He died prematurely and before Jesus could reach him. What do you do when you are dead? Stay dead? Come back? Most would of course want to come back, but how is that done? How do you come back from the dead? Death is supposed to be the end, the conclusion, the termination, the point of no return, no recall, no reversal; it is said to be the ultimate shut down. Perhaps that is how you feel; dead. Dead in one, two, or all areas of your life. Conclusion: all hope is lost, the door is closed, locked, and the key thrown away.

Lazarus died and was buried; there is no contention of that fact. But that's not how the story ends. Jesus soon arrived, and like the mighty king and fearsome warrior that he is, called out in a loud voice, "Lazarus, come forth!" and without hesitation, Lazarus walked out of the door of death, the door no one exits. Not because it was a natural thing, but because the creator of nature decided to suspend some of its laws. Do you know what? He is saying the same thing even now. He's standing outside the dead-end doorway of your loss and he's saying, "Turn around and come out!" You too can be out. Don't let your past hold your future hostage! There is no such thing as impossibility when it comes to the God of all creation. You most purpose in your heart, I'm coming out!

The reason we recognize and revere heroes is because they did not quit. Even if their own mistakes precipitated a personal disaster, some how, they found a way to initiate a magnificent turnaround and made a "come back". My view of a hero is not just one who conquered and never failed, but also those who clawed their way back from the abyss of failure and despair, and moved on to excel. Tough times are the wombs that nurture and birth heroes, and failure is often the incubator that hatches success.

"And what shall I say? For the time would fail me to tell of Gideon and Barak and Samson also of David and of Samuel and the prophets: who through faith subdued kingdoms, worked righteousness, obtained promises, stopped the mouths of lions".

Heb.11:30

Isn't it amazing to know that Samson's name made the list of those mighty men of God who are called heroes of faith? I think it is not just amazing, it is also inspiring! How long Samson waited to make the one good decision that reversed his course even in blindness is immaterial, the important thing is that he came back and in a big way for that matter. Sin caused his name to be dusted off, but he refused to stay down and out, he sprang back despite his incapacitation!

Sometimes bad things happen to you not really because you did anything to cause them or deserve them. But more often than not our suffering can be traced to our own wrong decisions, wrong motives, selfish desires, or foolish choices. Which ever way they come through, the undisputable fact is that we are bedeviled everyday by sundry problems. It doesn't matter whether yours is a physical, spiritual, relationship, mental or financial setback. If it's broken it needs to be fixed. If it's missing, lost or stolen, it needs to be found or replaced. If it is tainted, scattered, battered or abused, it needs to be restored. You need to know and accept that there is a restoration road map for you, whether from a decade-long sentence as in Samson's case or from a day-long detour from the path of righteousness and purpose as it often happens to us. No matter how far you've gone in your aberration, or how long you have stayed wallowing or trapped in the sticky situation, if you listen you will hear the father saying 'you can never be so far gone that my long hands cannot reach out and bring you back on the right path to your destiny'.

Is there really a way back?

The fact that you are still here and reading this book tells me your story is not finished yet. But as you read these words, perhaps you are experiencing a rerun of bad memories and it seems the world is cold against your skin. Maybe you feel stripped and dried-out with no roots to brace yourself with, no place to go and no one to lean on. You feel like a tree detached from the soil that could or would provide substance or nutrients. Listen my friend; Life's road takes a lot of twists and turns. It is fast one moment and slow the next, complete with unexpected hairpin curves and exhilarating acceleration down straight stretches. Then there are those times when life comes to a complete stand still, a dead halt. You reach a dead end.

A bad decision at a previous fork in the road has brought you to that place. You must not throw in the towel, or look for a possible short cut that you might think should be there somewhere, this is what you must do; shift your life's gears into reverse. Then begin the inch-by inch retreat in backward motions to a place where you can make your corrections and return to the proper path. No matter how far you have gone amiss, the only way out is a u-turn. God does allow u-turns you know. That you are behind the curtains does not mean the opera is over! It is time for a curtain call.

Samson's hair was cut off which is symbolic of his strength for ministry being taken away. His eyes were removed, which is a picture of his vision for ministry being blinded. Men mocked, reviled and made jest of him. He became a symbol of reproach and shame with no place to hide his face. In the process Samson learned a vital lesson; that the arm of flesh does fail, but also that you can never be so deeply buried in whatever situation or circumstance may have engulfed you that the resurrection power of God cannot bring you back. He prayed for his strength to be renewed, God answered him, and scripture records that he destroyed more enemies in his death than in his life time. When men are trying to run you down because of the mistakes you made, don't try to put up a defense. They are just indirectly advertising you! Let nothing hold you back. Your hair can grow again! You are finishing strong!

"Better is the end of a thing than its beginning"

CHAPTER 2

OH GOD WHY AM I HERE?

"And it came to pass, on the morrow that Moses went into the tabernacle of witness; and, behold the rod of Aaron for the house of the Levi was budded, and brought forth buds, and blossoms, and yielded almonds"

Numbers 17:8

All of this happens at the very place and time that the almond tree must have felt most abandoned, broken, and so alone as we read from God's most holy word. That most lonely place where you hit some pothole and felt may just be a place God has taken you to remodel you so you can be compliant to his plans for your destiny. He can raise you up again on that same on going axis, or move you somewhere else to carryout his divine plan. But He can never abandon you.

Some years back I lost my accommodation because the landlord asked me to leave his house. I met a pastor and asked if he could let me stay in one of the rooms in his apartment until I found my feet. He asked me rather to go and live inside his church. I accepted his offer and was sleeping in the church on the floor, most times without food to eat and no one to talk to. I was grateful to him but yet I cried because that was not what I had trusted God for. Inside of me I felt so reduced and tarnished, I was almost sure something was wrong with me. This church was located on D close of the estate. Today I live on the C close of that same estate in Lagos and God has blessed my hands and my ministry. It was in the same river Peter worked all night without success, that he netted the miraculous fishes. That same marriage will work out! That same womb will produce a baby. That same location will yield fruits. Don't go by what you see now. The devil is afraid of your tomorrow, much more than you think.

God told Moses in the scripture above to lay up the rods in the most holy place right in front of the Ark of the Covenant "Where I will meet with him". When Moses laid the dead and discouraged rod of Aaron in the darkness of the most holy place, the rod must have been alarmed. It may have thought like you and I, 'why would my master abandon me in what seems to be a lifeless place? Why was I brought to this place of punishment, a place for the disposal of unwanted things?'

Here is where we, along with the almond tree must understand; when our dreams are dying, God's plans are often just beginning. One night in Gods presence and you can become what you always dreamed you were supposed to be. Supernatural habitation trumps dark desperation. Something greater is at work here, it is called the "shadow of the almighty"

Revival and total come back can only happen when we are laid up in the presence of God. This is all you need when you feel stripped, dry and disconnected from what matters to you the most.

Have you ever struggled to understand why it seems God picked you up bare and plop you outside your comfort zone? Have you told yourself or anyone else who cares to listen 'I'm drying up! Something is missing and I have to be reconnected. I need to get my root back into the soil; I need to get back to the stuff that used to make me happy? Be careful, life isn't about the soil of our earthly existence or even the rays of the sun. It is all about God's dwelling place. The shadow of the almighty!

Wait in His Presence

One night in God's presence can accelerate your destiny beyond your craziest imagination. If a day is "as a thousand years, and a thousand years as one day" before our God, then do you know He can take a thousand years worth of blessing, compress it, wrap it up and infuse it into your life in one day?

I don't know how long you've suffered with the fear that your life was drying up, and the feeling that you were gradually but inexorably being cut off from your destiny. Life really can sometimes leave you feeling like firewood stacked up and waiting for the painful oblivion of the flames. It may be difficult for you to fathom, given the pain and confusion attending your present circumstances, but believe me, even during those moments when you feel ignored, isolated, abused, shamed and abandoned, God's presence is there. Take comfort in the promises of God. He knows exactly where you are!

Now, I know you'll say to me it's easier said than done, and I whole heartedly agree with you, but that hardly subtracts from the undeniable and irrefutable truth that if you wait on the lord, even when you feel "laid up" in dim isolation, you will gain new strength, life will spring up again, and things will happen even while you appear to be disconnected from all of your natural source of life and strength.

People will look at you and say: "how did that come from your life? You aren't even connected the right way!" "Nobody predicted you would do this well. You just don't have the credentials or experience for this! The rain didn't come into your life how come you are here blooming and producing fruits". This is what the lord will do for you and your critics. It is time to lay every thing down in the presence of the almighty. He will impact your life when you lay down your life in his presence and wait.

David said "thou at my hiding place" have you ever been hidden by God? Kept in a place of isolation, away from the pleasures you crave so much? Then your total restoration is sure! For, only an intimate encounter with his presence can resurrect your dreams and restore you to your destiny for which you were born. Just one powerful moment of total intimacy and God can resurrect your dead dreams, ministry, job, marriage, and projects. Never underestimate the potential of an encounter with God's presence! That soil is not your source. I pray that the light of his word dawn on your path.

Perhaps you feel forgotten, like a child's broken and useless toy packed in an old chest to rot away in the attic or stuffed in the closet of forgetfulness. You may doubt that I have even an inkling of how stripped and naked you feel, and do you know what? You may somehow be right. But it is not my understanding of how you feel that really matters here, it is my knowledge of how God feels about you: to give you a future and a hope: to beautify, adorn, garland and then plant your future, your tomorrow, your destiny on a sure, unshakable, immovable and irremovable foundation, to make you and showcase you as a praise and the crowning glory of his creation. You may even be taking it out on "all those hypocritical" authors, preachers, and the super testimonies of other folks trumpeting God's faithfulness, but please don't, it will be your turn soon to write a whole symphony on the same theme. People may tell you, "you cannot grow unless you have the light of the sun, the approval of the higher powers of the land shining on you" the truth under heaven is that only one power, the power of Jehovah matters, and the favor and the approval of this power which outshines all others is beaming on you, maybe right now from behind the clouds. Just wait a little, look, the clouds are clearing, and the gloom is lifting. Don't resent the very circumstances God has sent to develop you; wait in His presence.

At a time in my life and ministry I was hard put shaking off the feeling that I had missed God. I felt like I had committed the worst sin on planet earth and the judgment of God was being visited on me, as the storms raged out of control and things began to fall apart in my ministry. Gradually I sold out all we had in ministry and prepared to fold up. The pastors who came to purchase our musical instruments now had me as their new sermon topics and illustrations; the classic example of a man who failed in ministry because either he was not call of God or was living a double standard life.

But while the situation caused people to slap their thighs in derision, it was dragging me to God's presence to ask important questions about my life. I went to Abuja in the year 2004 and attended a ministers' conference where Dr John Akpami preached on "failure is referable" and that brought a total turn around in my whole life. Today the same set of pastors fear and bow their heads in silence when they see me in their midst. I am almost sure that when they see me on television preaching they wonder if it is me or some one else. The dry bones can rise again. I have learned never to allow my past take my future hostage. And never have I again interpret life through the eyes of my circumstances. A man may be down now but don't write him off; doesn't the sun go down? Did it ever remain down? You may have seen him drown before your very eyes, and the next moment you see him come riding out on the crest of a wave or farfetched as it might seem, on the back of a dolphin. Who can understand the implements the almighty chooses to work with? God wants to make you a testimony for the world to see! Trace your way back to that place of intimacy and re-establish your contact with Jehovah your God, for the best parts of your testimony are developed in His presence.

There is a man of God in Nigeria who at a time became or seemed to have become insane. Every one mocked the preacher who as it were had gone mad, eating from the dust and waste bins. Folks in mockery said "the demons he cast out have come after him and overpowered him". But that man has one of the greatest deliverance ministries in Nigeria today. Don't write any one off. I may be seen to be washing my nets like the apostle Peter in Luke 5:2, and to others it may seem like a sign saying 'packing up', but for me it is for the purpose of throwing them back.

You may have gone through hell and all who use to respect you are now making mockery of your person. Don't forget, nothing dies in God's presence. By divine design, the manna that God provided for the Israelites in the wilderness could not keep overnight. When the rule was broken, maggots infested the manna; it stank and was no more edible. However, the manna Aaron placed in the Ark of the Covenant stayed permanently fresh and alive, because it was to be a visible witness to the provision of God to generations who knew nothing about the fourth-years wilderness journey.

> *"And Moses said to Aaron, take a pot and an omer of manna in it, and lay it up before the lord, to be kept for generations. As the lord*

commanded Moses, so Aaron laid it up before the testimony, to be kept"

Ex 16:33-34

The presence of God was the source of energy and power that infused life into the dead almond tree branch causing it to bud and not merely the box or the tent where they kept it. It is not about the "farm" where you are planted; it's about the "farmer" who planted you. Nothing dies, rots or stinks in His presence. Your fragile dreams, your delicate constitution, your limp personality, your comatose marriage, life and ministry will download strength and stay permanently fresh in the presence of God.

When every one around you says "your dream can't come true, you can't get out of this evil rumor against you, do you remember you told lies yesterday? What about that lady you slept with who is not your wife? When the stress and demands of life leave you wondering if you are not better off dead, pay deaf ears to them, press into His presence and stay there until you are renewed again. Freshness and strength to face life with zest is a by-product of God-man intimacy.

You may have been stripped of all protection, integrity and life-giving resource. It's possible you've lost everything and become disconnected from everything that could give you energy to go on. When there's no where else to turn, find yourself in His presence. The genesis of your restoration is an encounter with the presence of God. The maintenance of your restoration is connected to continued exposure to God's presence. Scripture says "The name of the lord is a strong tower; the righteous run into it and are saved" You are never so wrung out or dry or lost that the life giving moisture of God's presence cannot find you, freshen you up, and restore you to your rightful place in God's economy. No matter how stripped and bare you are, a day in his presence will leave you warm, clothed and dignified. Find the presence and stay there.

CHAPTER 3

DON'T COME IN, I'M NAKED!

"And the lord took man, and put him into the garden of Eden to dress it and to keep it. And the lord God commanded the man, saying, of the tree of the garden thou mayest freely eat: But of the tree of the knowledge of good and evil, thou shall not eat of it. For in the day that thou eatest thereof thou shalt surely die. And they were both naked, the man his wife and were not ashamed"

Gen 2:15-17, 25.

"And the serpent said unto the woman, ye shall not surely die. And the lord God called Adam, and said unto him, where are thou? And he said, I heard thy voice in the garden, and I was afraid, because I was naked; and I hid myself."

Gen 3:4, 9-10

God's dream for us is that we mirror the glory and the character that He possesses. He created man in His image and likness, authorizing him to rule and have dominion over everything on the earth just like He Himself does in heaven. So when you walk with Him in obedience you give him the excuse to bless you, just as disobedience can be God's permission to curse you.

Adam the first man God created and gave a wife and a garden to keep, is a type of the ministry today. He was created without sin. He had the real nature of God. One would think a man created with a nature like his to be a superman. Considering he was a fresh product of the power of creation he should be above falling into sin. But this was not the case as we read of this God's first created son. He fell at the very first appearing of sin and temptation upon his ministry.

Dressing the garden and naming the animals, was his first place of assignment. Why should he fall? Is it because he was new in ministry, still in the first phase of his work and walk with God? This is a puzzle that you may have to wait till eternity's drums roll, to solve. Though this can make us ask 'so who can stand?' it does not negate the fact that the name of the lord is able to keep us save until His appearing.

Adam fell out of the move of God for his life and ministry. His ministry was cut short because the devil, the enemy of the church entered unchecked into the camp! A little leaven, leaventh the whole lump, says scriptures it becomes very important therefore that we "Bring out the little fox that spoils the vine. For our vines have tender grapes" as another wisdom nugget from scripture advices. We must close and lock the back doors of our ministries, plug and block every opening that may allow the devil entry into our domain, lest we fall prey to the devil's assaults."

I have often asked; why should a man of God fall into sin? Why should God's holy ones be mocked in the mud? Why should the saints of God face shame while working for the lord? The truth is it should not be so; but sad to say, it is.

The on going satanic revival against the church and the saints is the passion behind my writing this book. Truly we don't want to lose focus of our walk with God nor do we want to betray the trust the father has on us, but then we find ourselves caught in the web of uncertainty and shame and we can't place what is really happening.

Can it Be?

> *But while men slept, his enemy came and sowed tares among the wheat, and went his way.*
>
> Matt 13:25

Can it be because the church is sleeping? Oh yes of course it is possible! What with the bride of the lamb so preoccupied with aesthetics, politics, titles, and positions, so given to performing for society's applause and perishable things, so taken with internal wrangling, strife, gossip, malice, bickering and petty jealousies; what with a situation where the contention is so much ministers cant see eye to eye, where the message of the cross which is the power of God unto salvation is relegated to the background, while the philosophies of men make the waves, it is a highly disturbing scenario. What gives me the frights is that it does not seem like the church is aware that there is a fearsome battle raging in which she is deeply embroiled in. The devil must be mocking our ignorance, while the holy angels watch in great dismay as the beautiful image of the church falls to the tricks and traps set to destroy her, for in this her slumbering state, who would stop the wily thing even if it came marching in with drums rolling and banners flying?

> *"The weapons of our warfare are not canal, but mighty through God to the pulling down of strong holds"*
>
> 2Cor. 10:4.

We need to rise up, make a holy call mobilizing the saints to stand up, fight this evil sprite that vexes us all and send it with its evil life style back to Satan where it came from.

The devil is ready to pay any price to put the church to sleep so that he can have an unhindered passage as he carries out his mission of devastation on earth. We must not let that happen. We need to stop throwing stones at one another, start making sacrifices on behalf of the church, laying down our lives for each other as the command from our God entails and refuse the enemy any foothold on our land. It is time for war!

Instead of standing aside to watch, or trampling each other to death, let us lift one another up both spiritually and physically. None of us must be left to the mercies of the enemy. I plead we take hid to the counsel Paul the apostle gave in Hebrews 13:1 "Let brotherly love continue" Standing together we will be an utterly invincible army.

Adam was naked in the garden. He must have felt so all alone in the fight. His wife, the one who was supposed to be the help meet for him, was the one who heralded the move for his fall. Many times the ones we least expected would harm us are the tools the devil uses to frustrate us. And a man's foes shall be they of his own household says the wise man in Mtt.10:36.

Do you feel exposed? Does it seem like the whole world is gloating at your nakedness? Do you feel so all alone as folks with stones in their hands and hate in their eyes crowd you in, ready to lynch you? Every where you turn it's like there's so much evil being peddled about you that you don't feel like coming out again, right?

A woman was caught in the web of adultery and brought to Jesus. The elders of the church desired her death even more than the devil did. They would be fulfilled to watch her die in the pool of her own blood. Yes, because she was caught in the very act! But where was the man who slept with her.? There are many who would love to watch another person, maybe a fellow minister, die. That is all they long for! So, any mistake the person makes become a weapon in their hands. They enjoy publishing others in the media if they fall. What caused the fall is of no consequence to them.

Adam did not want God to come close to him because he had fallen. But God was just by his side. He is the almighty his voice dries up the mighty waters. He is closer than you think. He was so close that Adam heard His voice when He called.

There are folks you would never talk against if you knew how long the devil has been waiting to see them fall. Every one of us has at one time or the other been bitten by the power of failure and backsliding. I have had a lot of setbacks in ministry, marriage and even relationship with folks, but over the years in my walk with God, I have learned like I mentioned earlier, never to interpret life through the eyes of my circumstances.

No disrespect is intended, but can you imagine how innocent the elders of the church looked, until Jesus said "let he that is without sin cast the first stone?" don't we also put on those same airs; stony faced, dignified, self righteous, high and mighty defenders of the faith, when some one else's case has to be looked into? The woman longed to see a friendly face, but all she saw was the stones: stony faces and stone filled hands. Saints, what is our prize for a soul? Do you know that some one truly died for this? The true answer to this question is the spark needed to stir up the fire of revival; I pray that it does.

Jesus told her "go and sin no more" never had she seen such love in any other eyes. When a brother or sister falls into sin, do you join the crowd to say crucify him? Or do you say "go and sin no more" your true reaction to this will be based on the value you place on a soul.

Many of us have fallen, and are now naked. Many of us truly love the lord hence the devil looks out for us and we have been forced to play in this demonic drama a part we did not audition to play.

If Adam could fall, then we sure need the power in the prevailing blood of the lamb, Jesus to fight against the wiles of the devil. "For by strength shall no man prevail"

You may have been trampled upon, but if bitterness does not affect your spirit, then it cannot affect your destiny. For the anchor holds in spite of the storms!

When Adam fell, he was told to leave the garden, a type of God's presence. Samson fell out of God's power and was turned into a donkey-man to roll the grinding machine in the camp of his enemies. David sinned and war broke out in the land. You may have sinned too and found yourself floundering around, and broken. Such is the devastating power of sin, but in the midst of this I hear the voice of the master calling "let he that thirst come to the water"

The enemy was mighty he came in like a flood but he will be defeated by one drop of the blood that fell at Calvary. The reason why there is tomorrow for you in ministry is because God has not finished with you yet. God becomes more real when your life becomes a testimony.

If you dare to believe then miracles will happen. Mountains still move you know, demons still flee at the mention of the name of Jesus. The God that we serve is much more than able to save. No matter what any body says, don't be afraid just stand up and say. I DARE TO BELIVE! If you can run into God's presence he will expand your ways of thinking until folks look at you in that same place where they wrote you off and they will wonder at the power of change that has come upon your life.

Maybe folks thought you were washed out; they thought they would now control your life and ministry seeing that you are out of favor with God. But he is that God who makes the wounded strong again! No man can pluck you out of his mighty hands. "Under your slippery feet are his everlasting hands!" Last week you where crying, but hang on! He will prepare a table before you in the presence of your enemies.

For this reason also I will counsel you to make friends this year based on your intended destination if you must get to the finishing line, because not every body is headed in the direction of your destiny this year. Don't permanent a relationship that God is terminating! Don't choose your friends until you are on the cross with a mocking thief by your side, and the earth underneath you rejoicing at your fall. Only then will you know who your friend truly is. Hey, I hear the lord say, "drop that Hammer in your hands because you are slaying the wrong lamb."

Behind the Glass Door

The time has come when we should go to the enemy's territory and take back what he stole from us! Get ready to be released from the shackles that chained you to the prison walls of the predictable, allow God to place in your hands the keys that un-lock the door to the emerging prophetic order of the saint that you are!

We have been given the gospel of repentance and love; we have got to declare this gospel with sure boldness! People can only die for the sake of the gospel if they know the gospel is worth dying for. I say this because I think we have made the gospel so unrealistic it has caused more people too stumble and fall than to stand. I am referring to our modern gospel of hypocrisy and white washed sepulchers. The world outside our church walls views Christianity as a holier-than-thou religion full of charlatans who preach a plastic gospel of "do's" and don'ts.

I believe the gospel of the bible must be preached without compromise, and that we must show ourselves as becomes ministers, good examples of the brethren. But I have also found that our greatest ministry comes out of brokenness and transparency about our failures and pain. I am of the opinion that God does not even release us to minister to others until we have been broken on his alter of consecration and have come through the process with a good attitude.

We don't need to rush ahead of Gods timing. We need to stay on course with God until we are able to stand strong in our brokenness and say "let me share with you about the time I made the same mistake in my life and about how God corrected it" it is high time we came forward in total transparency and admitted before our congregations and those who look up to us how we struggled and are still struggling with some issues, so that they know they have to pray for us more. Don't be superman. You need God's help!

Most times pastors who have fallen into adultery or some other moral problems will go to other church leaders and confess their sinful acts. They claim to have been broken by their experience; the same inner weakness that led you to sin will lead you there again until the day it is totally broken. It is my responsibility to be the most transparent leader in the church because I expect it of the leaders under me. Being in touch with the REAL makes you a better minister.

If I never shared my failure and weakness with people, they wouldn't think I had any credibility to talk to them about any such things. I tell them how God saved me, how I failed my exams and later passed it. How the devil walked into my home and marriage. I tell them that I am a walking miracle, who is still in awe of the fact that God could chose to use me.

In the home too many of us are stranded arrows who were forced to start all over again. "Your grandmamma got divorced, you mama got divorced, so are you" "my granddad was broke, my dad was broke, and so am I" some how, somewhere, somebody in the blood line has to stand up for the occasion in Christ and say "enough! The curse stop right here, and right here is where Gods blessing beings"

The best way to give God all the glory is to tell the bad side of the story too. To try to make them think you were a virgin on your wedding day when you know what happened in the back seat of the car one cold evening, is a self deluding enterprise that brings you no income. Tell them it wasn't worth it! Tell them the truth! Tell them what you have been through so they won't have to suffer the same pain needlessly. Explain to them how God has moved you and what you have learned in the process. Then watch them, because they need your help. Don't let your living, your pain and your mistakes be in vain. Preach and teach it out, let it help someone; that is ministry!

How do you feel when you are found wanting to defend or trying to repair the gospel you once preached? You who once preach against fornication and abortion, castigating, lambasting, and mercilessly cutting down anyone who was even hinted as having perpetrated such a shameful and unthinkable act and casting doubt on the veracity of their claim to being born again, are you now sneaking out money to facilitate the abortion of the seed you wrongly panted in sin? Can you see that anyone could have fallen into that same or any other sin? So now what are you going to do about it? Your love for people should be evident and unconditional. Love them, hug them, and openly show them you care, especially when they have done wrong. Show them that your ministry is not that of condemnation, but that of reconciliation. Showing Jesus love for others should be our motivation for ministry. Remember, he loved prostitutes and sinners, and didn't mind showing it in front of every one.

People even our children can relate better to those who are transparent about their failures and short comings. We should allow our brokenness and our scars of failure become a visible testimony to God's power and willingness to deliver and transform us. God delights in using broken people to bring wholeness and deliverance to others.

God chose David although he was an adulterer and murderer. He chose Moses to confront pharaoh although he was a murderer with a serious speech impediment. He chose Paul although he was a highly trained Pharisee and one of the most dedicated persecutors of the church. The problem with church folks is that too many of us are looking for another Jesus in the pulpit. I am human enough to err! But he is God enough to forgive me, correct me and lead me in the part of righteousness. He will never leave my soul in hell!

Satan counts it a great achievement if he can make a great man of God undress himself before a little maid, talk more of sleeping with her. But if the man of God leaves it there, the devil has won. If however because of that blunder the man of God decides that no one else as long as he lives will make the same mistake, the tables are turned on the enemy, and hell regrets that it ever caused the man of God to sin, just like if he knew, he would have done everything in his infernal power to stop Jesus going to the cross. Thank God he didn't.

Posing to be without fault is like the story of the emperor who because of his pride and arrogance walked the streets naked in clothes supposedly visible only to holy eyes. It is like closing and locking a transparent glass door to undress.

CHAPTER 4

FIRMNESS UNDER FIRE!

THERE IS A false tendency to believe that if we are surrounded by people, we will no feel lonely. Funny but true, you can be surrounded by an amphitheatre full of people bearing truck loads of accolades and yet be left feeling lonely.

Have there been instances where those who received and welcomed you with high esteem, turned around to debase you in public for one reason or another? Perhaps you failed to live up to their expectations. Now you have become an object of spite they must ignore and keep at arms length. You, the same person that they use to affirm or respect, now an outcast? It is a hard bone to chew. It would weigh even the most stout hearted of men down. This is the kind of stuff from which depression is born.

We all at one point or the other in our lives have tried to conquer depression. Every one in the bible who was close to God did. At one time the psalmist feeling very depressed cried out:

> *"Save me, o God; for the waters are come in into my soul. I sink in deep waters, where the floods overflow me. Am weary of my crying: my throat is dried: mine eyes fail while I wait for my God."*
>
> Psalm 69:1-3.

Many times situations threaten to overwhelm and snuff life out of you. When the waters, in the time of trouble, flow into your spirit, it brings to bear the plan and purpose the devil on your life. It is a daily victory you have got to win. Because Satan will throw everything he's got at you until your normal appetite for food or anything that gave you pleasure and joy is lost. He will fight you until he brings you down on your knees, doubting yourself, your salvation and your loved ones. He will attack your body and your mind so bad you may end up in the hospital. He wants to destroy your life; that is why he is after you. You must not let him invade the privacy of your spirit because

> *"The thief cometh not, but for to steal, to kill, and to destroy...."*
>
> John 10:10.

Depression means that your spirit is down and you have lost touch with brightness. It means that what should stay outside in now staying inside. This means you are withdrawing, breathing in water instead of air. Depression causes you to do what you would not do on a normal day. It makes you an associate of folks you normally would have no business getting along with. The fastest way to missing your way is to follow those who are lost; you will have no problem getting lost as well. That is what depression does.

In Job 3:11 we read these despairing words

> *Why did I not die from the womb? Why did I not give up the ghost when I came out of the belly?*

This is a great depth of depression. Job was depressed because he had lost his family, wealth, friends and contacts. You know, when you go through hard times it is much easier to bear if you have someone to lean on. Satan loves to isolate you and make you feel or see that you are the only one going through this kind of stuff. His plan is to help you destroy yourself. But listen beloved of God, the devil cannot kill you; he cannot wipe you out because he does not have the capacity, the power or the authority to do so. (That is why you cannot charge him for murder!) But he can help you kill yourself! Job's wife told him "curse God and die" his friends looked at him for eight days and said no word to him. This is atmosphere for depression complete with garnishing.

In the book Numbers Chapter 11 we see Moses reacting to depression. Moses was depressed because of the attitude of the people toward him and God. Jonah was depressed when he sat under the tree in realization that his plans had failed. Peter was burdened after denying the lord. Prophet Elijah, a powerful man of God hid under a tree in a state of depression over what he had lost. Later he ended up in a cave wishing he were dead simply because he thought he was going through a crisis alone. This is the same Elijah who saw the manifestation of the hand of God on the mount Camel when he called down fire now running for his life from a woman by the name of jezebel. This is depression. It turns you into what you are not. Have you ever found yourself under a tree or in a cave despairing of life itself?

Elijah allowed himself to succumb to a false alienation ploy. Sometimes it is when we are visited by rejection from those we expected to love us in return and we can humbly look out of the sphere of pain and rejection we are in, that we would realize that God never leaves any of His children alone.

Elijah wanted to die but God was not ready to assist him in that venture. Elijah had a touch of what I call cirrhosis. This is a place where you don't want to relate with any body. It is a place of self distortion, a place where you've lost contact with reality.

I don't know if you have come to that point in your life where you are all by yourself, and you feel so isolated. Elijah said "I'm the only one who has not bowed to Baal" he had lost touch with reality at this point.

Some times the help and comfort you need may not come from the source you expect but look beyond the usual to discern and trust God for the unusual. Depression affects your self image. That is why you don't want to cut or make you hair any more, you don't want to fix your nails any more, even when your dresses are not clean or good looking you still want to put them on. Most time under this depressive rage you don't feel like talking to any one, take your bath, eat your food or even look at the mirror to make yourself up in fact you even hate the sight of yourself. You just want to give up and die! You look so bad that people start asking "what is wrong with you? This is depression.

Dear reader, you are not alone in that night season of life, you are not alone facing that divorce, and you are not alone raising your children. Elijah in the cave of depression received a word of assurance that brought about motivation to move ahead and get by with life and its limitations. Listen there's a word coming for you.

Trying very hard to impress somebody brings depression. Trying to make somebody love you can bring depression as well. You are hurt that's why you are lashing out those words that are saucy and programmed to hurt; words that you won't say to any one on a good day. Because that is the only way you feel you can express yourself and release those poison from your mouth and heart, you just let go. Hmm.

It is not on an easy street that you become a power house or a house hold name. You have got to go through some stuff before you can become what you dream to be. You may be down but you are not out. You lost you car, house, love ones, and friends have walked out on you? Don't give up!

It is one thing to be in trouble and blame yourself and another thing to be in trouble and know it's not your fault! It is better to suffer when people are comforting you than to suffer when there is no one to lean on. Most times the place you should have gone to receive consolations, your religion forbids you going there. Like the case of the woman with the issue of blood as we read in the bible. In her time the law of the land forbade a woman with the flow of blood to touch a man.

Have you ever been in a church needing God and folks look you in the eye and you know, though their mouths are not moving, that they are saying you "what are you doing here, people like you don't come here"

There are troubles you can keep secret and there is trouble that calls attention to itself. Some time you make it through the private troubles but now here you are locked up with problems that the public knows about and you begin to feel so isolated.

Some times you shut the door from the outside but you can't shut the pain that is in the inside. The pain from the inside can kill you fastest. Here you are by yourself dealing with issues you did not bring on yourself. You have been forced by time and season to sit for an examination you did not register to write, and folks who should have helped you out are not fort coming.

You are crying to yourself; you wish you had some body who can cry with you. You are trying to keep it

secret but it is taking too long for an answer or solution to come, and the task of keeping it secret is becoming even more herculean than the problem itself. Have you ever felt like every one has failed you, yet something tells you from the inside "don't give up"? You throw your baby on your husband and you want to walk away and some thing says, Hold on! "Beloved, he that comes after God must believe that he is the rewarder of them that diligently seek him" Heb. 11:6.

Some one says "I can never be any thing in life" don't go by your feelings; go by your spirit and what the lord is saying to you via his word. "It is not by might nor by power but by my spirit says the lord"

The woman with the issue of blood was a very determined woman with a weak and bleeding body. She was a tramp, a cast away, a vagrant, smelly and repulsive, but crawled her way to Jesus and touched him. God is the only one who can marry a tramp! Hey, have friends called you a tramp, did your family also call you a tramp, and as the days go by it seems you are having your worst nightmare manifesting in real life? Do you hear woe echoing in your spirit? It is for your sake I wrote this book! Don't give up. Too much of God has been invested on you. His blood was shared for your sake.

People wanted to stop the woman with the issue of blood just like they did to stop blind Bartimaeus. But they both of them at different times in different places made up their minds. The man said "hey I have got no family, no food, no business, no marriage, no home, no one to fall back to and you want me to shut my mouth? I will holler until my miracle comes! "Son of David, have mercy on me"! The woman snaked her way despite the pushing and the bumping, the insults and the pain that must have attended he venture. Both received their miracles.

Beloved, in our faith walk with God there is always a fight before you can get to the next level and the weight of the fight tells the capacity of the champion you need to beat to win and the higher the devils you wrestle down, the higher level you attain. Only the courageous are wining!

Jesus is the man who has seen it all. A man who has willingly died before does not fear death any more. Jesus died to curses turning them into blessings, his death shut up the sun, tore the veil in the temple from the top to the bottom, shook the heavens and the earth until the Roman soldier said "truly this man is the son of God", the thief by his side said "remember me when thou come into thy kingdom" and the grave opened her mouth in Jerusalem, by this death the bible declares now are ye the sons of God! Jesus paid it all for you. You don't need to carry it any more!

Christianity is a fight; those who are not ready to fight are not ready to live. The devil intends to put us off track but like Paul we have got to put in our best until we reach the end, finishing strong!

"wherefore seeing we also are compassed about with great a cloud of witnesses, let us lay aside every weight, and the sin which doth so easily beset us, and let us run with patient the race that is set before us, looking unto Jesus the author and the finisher of our faith: who for the joy that was set before him endured the cross, despising the shame, and is set down at the right hand of the throne of God"

Heb 12:1-2

Paul knowing truly well, that he had not arrived rightly said in phil. 3:13, 14. Brethren, I count not myself to have apprehended: but this one thing I do, forgetting those things which are behind, and reaching forth unto those things which are before, I press toward the mark for the prize of the high calling of God in Christ Jesus.

I pray that the enemy does not take away your affection from the one who has paid with his blood to redeem you. Millions of souls who have been trampled upon slip into hell daily and those who are of the house hold of faith suffer untold physical and emotional pain because of the way we have treated them. It is for such people we must live, for them we must breathe, for them we must give up the comfortable life the world offers us.

Friends while you are on earth, make it your life ambition to encourage those slipping from the faith, those who have been tramped upon by the storms of this world and bring them to the throne of God on that day when time will no longer be, and all of eternity will stretch infinitely before us.

Unless you have Gods perspective each day, pressure will always determine our priorities. God's sense of urgency differs from ours. God's greatest victory takes place at your darkest moment.

> *"And he said unto them, what manner of communication are these that ye have one to another, as ye walk, and are sad? And the one of them, whose name was Ceapas, answering and said unto him, art thou only a stranger in Jerusalem, and hast not know these days? And he said unto them, what thing? And they said unto him, concerning Jesus of Nazareth,*

> *which was a prophet mighty in deed and word before God and all the people"*
>
> Luke 24:17-19

This is the story of the Emmaus encounter. In three years of Jesus ministry he had upset the whole city.

The whole city was amazed at the deposit of the word of wisdom that flowed from him.

Here they were telling Jesus about himself. They were in the midst of answers but they were asking questions. They were with THE solution but were still wallowing in problems. He was the manna that fell in the wilderness they should have known him. He was the coat of skin that covered the nakedness of Adam, they should have known him. He was the voice that sounded like many waters they should have known him. He was the veil of the temple that tore from the top to the bottom, they should have known him.

You see folks will often get along with you until you change the tune they are used to hearing. As soon as you begin to change the pattern they have always identified you with, they say you have gone into error.

It amazes me when I hear people say "that man is in the wrong ministry, what he or she is doing is not what God called him to do" my question usually is, were you there when God called him or her, were you there when God gave him or her the pattern to follow? Please

no disrespect is intended. If you don't know what he was told to do, why should you draw a line against him?

Beloved, the last place you saw a man is not the best place to measure him with. A man could be beaten by a thief almost to the point of death, but he is not dead yet! He may be in that pool of blood now but that is not his capacity. Don't measure his strength by his pains for the now. Measure his strength by what God says about him. Because the hair of the fallen Samson grew back, the snails also entered the ark of Noah; the thief at the cross with Jesus also got saved! Any body can be saved, any body can be healed, and any body can bounce back again.

It is only the church that tramples on and kills her wounded and fallen soldiers, instead of helping them make it back home safely. God allows us to pass through some storms because of what he has for us. Most times God allows those troubles so that he can reveal himself to us and to let us know how much we truly need Him. And these problems will in the end reveal the real you as well. It seems to me like the church does not understand this principle, but thank God he has a way of always showing up in our darkest moment. We cannot be consumed.

God's ways are past finding out. His thoughts are not our thoughts. So keep doing what God told you to do. When God told Joseph that he was going to get to the palace, he never told him that there was also the pit and a prison he would necessarily be going through. The pit or the prison were not obstacles, the pit and the prison were God's way to the palace!

Friends, you may be on a dusty road now, but there is a high way ahead of you! Rejoice in the lord always and I again I say to you rejoice.

CHAPTER 5

The God Who Married A Tramp

IT WAS GOD who told prophet Hosiah to marry Goma in Hosiah 1:1. Why should a prophet marry a tramp like Goma? A prostitute with such a reputation. It was a really unheard of action Hosiah took, but the voice of God was behind this move. We cannot possibly place what was going on here with the prophet of God, when the bible counsels us not to be unequally yoked with unbelievers. But this is the way God will have him go if he must redeem his people. The spies who slept in the house of the prostitute, Rahab, as we read of the account of Joshua, they were people of God just like you and I.

God can use any thing, even a drunkard when the need so requires, to pass His message across to any one or nation. A time came that God had to speak through the mouth of a donkey. A donkey had to speak when there was no human voice to declare Gods intentions, when humans disobeyed God; he had to use an animal. Anything is a weapon in the hands of God.

The bible declares that God can raise up stones to praise himself. Don't throw that girl away, don't throw your son away, don't throw your wife or your husband out because of his or her error or misconduct. God needs them all. The blood was shared for all!

God's order or principles for breakthrough always follows the pathway of the breaking process. He took the bread, blessed it, broke it and gave it out like in Luke 24. He took Job from the city of Ur, blessed him with so much cattle and wealth, broke him with boils all over his body and gave him thereafter to pray for his friends. He took Moses from the loving arms of his mother, blessed him in the palace of pharaoh, broke him on the back side of the desert and gave him power to lead the children of Israel. He took Joseph from the caring arms of his father, blessed him in the house of Potiphar, broke him in the back side of the dungeon and gave him to feed his brothers. He took Paul from the Jewish court, blessed him with power to the point that he was healing the sick and casting out demons, break him inside the jail, and gave him to write most of the epistles that you are I are reading today. He took Jesus from the glorious city of heaven, the place of power and dominion, where the streets are made of gold and the walls of jasper, blessed him to walk upon the water of Galilee until the storms were slain by his word, feeding 5,000 people with few loaves of bread and fishes, break him on the cross and gave him to the dying world!

Not only did he do it to Moses, Paul, Joseph, or Jesus, at one point or the other in your life, God will either be taking you, blessing you, breaking you or giving you out. This is why I am not jealous of my friends or brothers who are blessed right now, because they may be going through a blessing process, while am going through a breaking process.

Messed up, don't give up! Too much of God has been invested in you. I thank God that He blessed me before he break me, if He had broken me before He blessed me, I would have died in that breaking process. But because He blessed me before He broke me, I know He once blessed me and am sure He will bless me again!

The glory of the later house will surely be greater then the former. Don't draw that line on me! Don't call it quite on me, don't call her a tramp! It is not about me but the blood Jesus paid for it all with! If you read about David and the wife of Uriah as told in scripture, you would want to kill David and draw that line about him, but this was the same David that God called "A MAN AFTER MY HEART"

Keep the fire burning! Folks may have called you all kinds of names with the view of mocking you, because of the gospel of the cross, press your way through. You may have fallen into all kinds of sinful acts so many times that now the church that was helping you out has thrown you away, don't give up! Press your way through like blind Bartimaeus.

How do you stop a woman with the issue of blood, with no family to fall back to, who has heard that Jesus is passing by? How do you stop the woman of Nain whose child is dead, and has gotten information that Jesus is coming to that same city? How do you stop the woman by the well of Samaria, whose marriage to over five husbands has not worked out, when Jesus is now asking her for a drink? How can anyone stop you when your set time is just around the Conner? Beloved, pressing for the mark of your high calling is needful now! The devil is after you and your ministry; you must not give him that opportunity he needs. Be ready to pour down your blood if need be when no one believes in what you are doing. You may be a tramp now, but Jesus came that you may have life, and have it more abundantly.

He is the God of the foolish, the God of the bad boys, the God who marries tramps! There are some folks you've got to call as you read this book and say to them "thank you for walking away from my life, thank you for cheating on me, thank you for betraying me, thank you for breaking my heart, thank you for running me down because of my mess, you have made me find Jesus. Am glad I went through it all alone. Am stronger now"

Hey Sarah, Isaac is on the way, listen Hannah, Samuel is on the way, are you there Elizabeth, John the baptizer is on his way, Mary, Jesus is coming hold on! Blind Bartimaeus, don't let anyone deter you, Jesus son of David will have mercy on you! The woman with the issue of blood, lift up your eyes, can you see? The hem is in front of you, don't let the crowd deter you, you are almost there. Friends, there is an ultimate come back for you, and it is here!

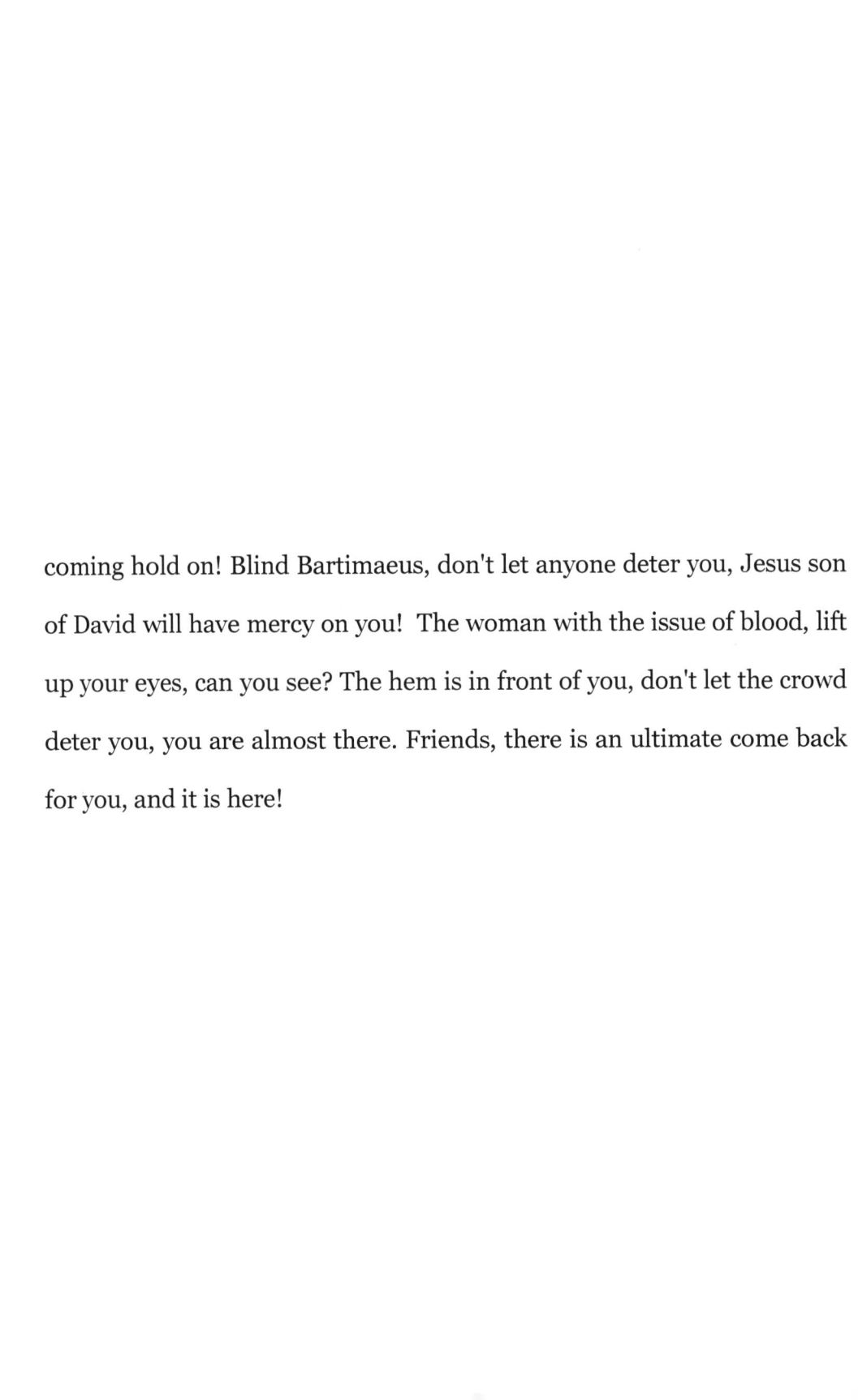

OTHER BOOKS BY THE AUTHOR

1. GIANTS ON SLIPPERY FLOOR

2. FRESH FIRE

3. ATTEMPTING THE FUTURE

4. BREAK THAT ALBASTAR BOX

5. CATCHING THE SPIRIT OF A LEADER

6. DOUBLE YOUR RESULT

7. PASSWORD TO FULFILING MINISTRY.

8: HELP, MY EMOTION IS FAILING ME.

9: KISS LABAN GOODBYE.

10: INTIMACY WITH GOD.

ABOUT THE AUTHOR

Apostle psalm okpe is an international renowned speaker , a gospel diplomat to the nations. His preaching impart has taken him to over 72 nations, a regular speaker to the United Nations in New York . An Ambassador of peace with the universal federation of peace under the United Nations. He holds a degree in philosophy and master in communications (university of American, Murrieta ,California) . He also holds a certificate in Human rights and international humanitarian law (from the institute of peace . Washington D.C)

He is the CEO of fresh oil Television broadcasting to over 108 nations daily. He is the founder and senior pastor of fresh oil ministry with many branches around the world . A television host of " The itinerary preacher " an author of 23 best selling books ; one of the most sought after speaker in conferences, seminars and crusade. He has made it possible for ministries and organizations around the world to accomplish great projects in estimates of millions of dollars and exuding the great grace of God working of miracles causing the lame to walk, the barren womb to bring forth babies , healing the sick and casting out Devils . He seats as the member of board of directors in many organizations and he is the CEO of 4 other companies

Made in the USA
Columbia, SC
13 September 2024